Ruby McGuill is an accomplished and talented author and storyteller. Her imaginative depiction of our Lord's birth and crucifixion, from the perspective of one we may call a bystander, is brilliant. Her insightful and heartfelt accounts of Christ's grace and sacrifice continue to touch the hearts of many. Ruby's gifts and talents have not been "hidden under a bushel," and her calling not ignored. I am sure the message within these pages will touch your life.

Willie Goldman   *Lake Charles, Louisiana*

Have you ever wondered what it was like to witness the birth and death of Jesus Christ? In "Cradle to Cross," Ruby McGuill shares her spirituality and creativity with the world. Her use of imagery, poetry, and storytelling coupled with an unexpected twist, make for a unique experience. As her characters came to life, my eyes and mind were opened to a perspective beyond imagination. She will do the same for you.

Vicki Childress   *Lake Jackson, Texas*

It is with great honor and enthusiasm that I present my endorsement of Ruby McGuill. I have known Ruby for many years and have observed the work of Jesus through her in different contexts. Ruby is very talented and creative and has a sincere heart for Jesus. She is a gifted vocalist and musician, an imaginative storyteller, and a woman of Christ-like character.

Rev. Ellis McKinzie   *Temple, Texas*

Bah humbug! I had lost the Christmas spirit…until *From Cradle to Cross for You* stirred something deep within me. What a brilliant and poignant portrayal of His birth and His ultimate sacrifice for you. When I think of Christmas, I now also think about grace and salvation. Ruby's unique way of portraying Jesus' birth and death touched my heart. Intertwining today's terminology and problems into a story 2,000 years old will bring smiles, chuckles and thankfulness while being reminded of the most glorious gift God has given us – our Lord and Savior! Thank you Ruby.

Jerry and Jeanie Hinkel   *Round Top, Texas*

I have known Ruby McGuill for several years, and have enjoyed her concerts and her reflections. She has the distinct ability to paint a picture with her words and make it come to life. Her stories touch the hearts of children and adults alike. I know Ruby believes in the Holy Spirit, who guides her life. I thank God that she has chosen to make these stories available to us all.

Rev. Deacon John McCourt   *La Grange, Texas*

FROM CRADLE TO CROSS
FOR YOU

FROM CRADLE TO CROSS FOR YOU

A Christmas Collection

RUBY McGUILL

XULON PRESS

Xulon Press
2301 Lucien Way #415
Maitland, FL 32751
407.339.4217
www.xulonpress.com

© 2019 by Ruby McGuill

Printed in the United States of America.

ISBN-13: 978-1-5456-7778-0

TABLE OF CONTENTS

FROM CRADLE TO CROSS FOR YOU

Today's story is the story of Christmas, but my story is also of a young boy named Maccabee. Have you heard of him? He was a simple teenage lad; the only child of Obadia and Martha who owned an inn in the little town of Bethlehem. Surely you've heard of Bethlehem. Let me introduce you to this precious family.

After a long trip from Nazareth, Mary and Joseph, tired and stressed, arrive at the Inn when the innkeeper we all remember said, "There is no room for you in the Inn." He had no room, but he offered a stable.

I choose to think this sweet man did the very best he could for the young couple. Could he help it that the Inn was full? It wasn't his fault, so he tried to make them comfortable. After all, how was he to know the young girl would deliver her first born child in THAT mess THAT night??? Mary, Joseph AND THEIR DONKEY, were ushered to the

1

stable where Obadiah and Martha brought sheets, blankets, clean water and anything Martha could think of to make them cozy. That was not an easy task given the situation. The difficult journey was reflected in Mary's face. Yet, beauty and peace radiated from her. Joseph tried to be a pillar of strength, but he too was weary.

Obadiah and Martha's teenage son, Maccabee, helped as well after finishing other chores. He was such a blessing to have around during these incredibly busy times. He was either in his wood shop, tending to animals or helping his father and mother. It seemed sometimes that he really never had a kid's life, but one of only hard work. He was so driven to be the best craftsman in the area, and many already thought of him as just that! Maccabee had GROWN MEN COMING TO HIM FOR ADVICE. It was a definite gift and he shared it with many. Furniture was his specialty, and it was always beautiful.

After the newlyweds were nestled as comfortable as possible under the stars, the family returned to the more normal chores of the evening... accommodating each guest with compassion and gratitude for their business. These two were natural born servants and definitely in the career they were meant to have. Obadiah served up generous portions for each resident's meal. And Martha, well, she was NEVER at a loss in finding ANOTHER chore to do or TO HAVE someone else perform. I can only imagine that today's B&B had nothing on them. After all, they cooked EVERY meal for EVERY resident EVERY day. McDonalds didn't exactly do breakfast then and Bethlehem was way too small for an I-HOP. Finally, Bethlehem's most popular Inn was beginning to settle down for the night.

Maccabee couldn't sleep for the hustle and bustle outside. There are so many weary travelers arriving in their little city for taxing. He kept thinking that the sweet couple in the stable must be incredibly uncomfortable. The young girl didn't seem much older than he was, and she was DEFINITELY GREAT with child!! Her eyes caught his just once as he brought them fresh bread and water. The beauty and peace in them spoke volumes to him. He just didn't understand why. She seemed to have wanted to say something, but so tired and weary from the long journey, she only kindly recognized his efforts to help them feel as relaxed as possible.

Who is she I wonder.
What is that young girl's name?
Her eyes shine with love unending.
Never have I seen the same.

Her husband serves her in love.
But, she must be very scared.
Yet, still she's demanding nothing.
So grateful for the straw-filled bed.

I pray they both rest well,
After such a journey trod.
Maybe tomorrow they can move inside.
'Tis my prayer Dear God.

Well, there is Dad's voice. "Goodnight Maccabee. Thank you for your help, and rest well son."

"Good night Dad. It was a good day."

Whew...I guess it really is time to call it a day, AND WHAT A DAY IT HAS BEEN!!

"I'm ready for these taxes to be collected and the STRANGERS TO LEAVE so I can get back to my wood-working. If I don't finish some of the orders and projects I have going, I'll NEVER have enough money for my own donkey. What girl is gonna wanna date a guy who can't even afford his own donkey? Oh well, for now, it's time for some quiet if possible. With all the decrees still echoing from my DEAR MOTHER and the stable animals bellowing, there are those in Bethlehem who may not sleep very well tonight. I, on the other hand, intend to get some shut eye. Good Night, Bethlehem!"

And with that, Maccabee relaxed in peaceful slumber.

"WHAT IN THE WORLD IS GOING ON OUT THERE? It's hardly dawn, but you can see for miles. There's this light from the sky like I've never seen. I feel like I'm waking up to some celestial choir in the distance. WHAT IS THAT SOUND?? This is really strange," Maccabee exclaimed as he awoke.

"Maccabee!!! Maccabee!!!! Please come down from the roof just as quickly as possible," his mother bellowed. "Your Father needs you down-stairs to help with breakfast. I'm going to be a bit tied up. The duties around this place ARE NEVER done! BUSY, BUSY, BUSY."

"Huh???? Ma'am????????? What's going on???" Maccabee mumbled.

"Your Father will fill you in," Martha ordered. "Just please please hurry!"

"Yes ma'am, I'm on my way." I sometimes wonder if I'll be here all my life.

"Hey Dad, what can I do to help?"

"Well Son," Obadiah stated, "Let's get coffee made and ready for the guests. Maybe we can have a cup also. I will fill you in on the events of the night."

They served the visitors and then sat down with a cup together and his father explained. "Maccabee, the young couple in the stable, Well, Mary had her baby last night, and now your mother thinks she's a grandmother. She is trying to help the young girl. Oh yes, baby and mama are both doing fine, just fine, but the circumstances are a little scary for a first time mom I'm sure. Joseph, the father, is beside himself with what to do. So YOUR MOTHER, SWEET SWEET MARTHA, IS TRYING TO SEE TO THEM THIS MORNING. I think the best thing we can do is tend to the other guests and stay out of her way."

"I'll do whatever I can to help out Dad, you know that. Do you think I could just go and see the baby for a minute? I promise I won't be long," Maccabee requested with excitement. Then he rushed to his shop.

There's no question he was on a mission. He uncovered a simple but beautiful cradle. The talented teen had made it some time ago from scraps left of a bigger job and it was PERFECT for a newborn. Away to the stable he went! With caution, he called out before he got to the entrance. "Mary.........Joseph????"

He then heard her quiet voice bid him in. Again, their eyes met. He knelt and sat the small cradle at her feet. Gently and softly, he filled it with straw

6

and watched. He watched as she lay the sleeping infant in HIS creation. His heart raced as he watched the baby sleep. EVERYTHING ABOUT THAT MOMENT was absolutely perfect!! The baby seemed so special and slept there in a cradle built by HIS OWN HANDS! HE SOARED WITH PRIDE!

Mary told Maccabee that she had named the baby "Jesus."

Life was never really the same at that little Inn. For MONTHS, visitors came to pay their respects to the newborn baby. Shepherds came from the fields outside of town. They simply wanted to see this baby. They had witnessed the same light in the sky that Maccabee had seen and it drew them to the stable. Later, Magi traveled from distant lands to bring expensive gifts to the baby boy. When they arrived, they knelt in reverence to the baby boy and literally seemed to worship Him. The gifts were gold, frankincense and myrrh. I'd never seen such treasures. It made me wonder why this baby boy was so incredibly special.

All this Mary treasured. She pondered it in her heart. At times, she just gazed into the heavens with a smile that simply made life at our house more peaceful. Joseph helped us tend some of the animals, and sweet baby Jesus grew stronger each day. Some days when I finished my work at the shop, I would go out and just rock the little cradle where He slept. Jesus gave me a new found inspiration for my woodworking. I was getting older as He was growing. I tried to give sweet Mary and Joseph a break, and I took Him to the shop to babysit occasionally. It was like HE WAS THE PERFECT CHILD!

Then one day, POOOOOOF....... They left! Mary, Joseph, and Jesus just packed up and headed out. It was like they were running from something, but I couldn't imagine what that might have been.

What a GREAT family I thought. I knew the motivation that little baby gave was inside me forever.

My business grew and with it a dream for bigger and better things. A nicer shop with a show room would be nice. A larger city with even MORE customer clientele was a dream too. Driven with new energy, I began to plan for just that. I used all the sources available to search for the perfect city. I began to utilize all my extra lumber, so I wouldn't have the excess to transport. Now.... It was time to let Dad and Mom know my plan. They really shouldn't mind. I'm beginning to be known as the "oldest bachelor in town" who STILL lives at mom's place.

"Dad, Mom... I've worked hard to build my business and I'm so thankful for all the trade that has come my way. I have some amazing and loyal customers, but my expertise is just not in high demand in Bethlehem and I will be moving on. I'd like to know that I have my parent's support in going to Jerusalem to open a larger shop. The town is bustling with people, the temple is there, and I just need a fresh start. I am willing to stay until you have someone who can help you. You guys aren't exactly spring chickens anymore ya know! Someday, I will be supporting a wife and family and I want to have security to offer them. Please let me know I have your blessing," Maccabee asked.

It took a while to organize everything. My plans to make the journey to Jerusalem were coming together. A new beginning.... Greater opportunity...New customers...More money...and YES, more SINGLE LADIES!! The ones around here are either married by now are more like sisters. We all grew up together and, well... You know what I mean.

Maccabee was ready. "It really shouldn't be a very long trip according to my sources." He assured his mother that he was still close enough to come home for visits and her home cooking occasionally. "I left with my donkeys packed to the hilt. I had bedding, tools, plenty of food for the trip and what lumber I still had from the last orders. It would help to get me started until I found a supplier." Here

I was…Young and free…Excited… and just a bit afraid of the unknown.

After one last hug, one more "I Love You," and every little detail Martha could think to cover, Maccabee was off to Jerusalem. It was bitter sweet, this move. The tears in his mother's eyes brought the same to his, but he would be back. Having his own business would allow for travel home for the holidays. He would even be able to take other trips back to help out during busy times at the Inn. His Mom and Dad stood at the door waving as he left.

The journey wasn't bad. "Wow… here I am in Jerusalem!" he thought. I'm not sure why we never visited this place as a family. It's really not a long trip. There are SO many people here! It's as if something really big is about to happen. I don't have the time to bother with crowds today. Now, to find a place for my animals and me. It would be great to discover home, shop, and barn… the whole works together. Does that sound selfish, but it could happen right? I will check the outskirts of town where I can secure a little more space for creating beautiful furniture for wonderful people."

SEVERAL YEARS PASSED AND LIFE GOT REALLY HARD.

"There are days I wonder why I still do this," Macaabee lamented. "I wonder if my parents had issues with each other like I do with my wife at times? The more successful I become, the more she spends. The more money I make, the more we seem to need. I love what I do, but the ends just aren't meeting. With money so tight, I am forced to buy lumber on credit at the local mills. Everyone wants something special and unusual; and that leaves me with more overhead than ever before. How on earth do I ever pay them back?" His doubts multiplied.

"Was it wrong to pick up and move here those many years ago? All of this stirs in my head constantly with no rest. Am I in too deep to leave? Where do I turn? I can't let my wife and children know how bad this really is. That would only cause more problems in our once happy home. I'm not sure I want or can do life without my wife and kids. Losing them over this would do me in. I've got to work something out."

I look back now and know, without a doubt. I know the one thing that can keep my head above water is the inspiration from that little baby Jesus. I've never forgotten those days.

Mary and Joseph were so gentle and loving to each other. I wish my wife were a little more like her; or maybe, I should be more like Joseph. I remember how he honored Mary. It was amazing to watch.

Oh well, let me get to work. There are all these people in town for the Jewish Passover. That always brings in some extra cash flow. These Jews can be pretty tight with their money, but small pieces may sell and transport easily. I CAN DO THIS! Maybe there IS a way I can satisfy the soldiers and buy myself some extra time in paying these debts in town. Maybe I can keep my family together. There's no one to do this but me and I need to "Just get'er done!"

It's off to town and to work out a deal. Passover is upon us and I have projects to complete.

"Oh my! You would think a king of some sort is coming to town," Maccabee exclaimed! "There are people EVERYWHERE!! Wait…There is a processional and these crazy Jews are hailing some man on a donkey! They are letting that nasty donkey walk on their clothing! I just can't believe this show!"

Perhaps I should check this out. Or maybe I should just be a little more social. Then, I would be aware of the events in our city.

And, "Who in the world is that guy on the donkey?" he wondered aloud.

Now I remember why I don't frequent the city. Oh no, he has seen me, that soldier that continues to hound me for money. I found out his name is Dave. He always said I shouldn't be purchasing on credit! But… why should he care? He doesn't own the lumber company, OR DOES HE? I would like to run, but there is nowhere to hide. Here he comes.

"Maccabee......Maccabee.......OVER HERE! We need to talk! Your debts are getting out of hand, and something needs to be done and soon! We won't allow this to continue," barked the soldier.

I'm thinking, what do I say? "Well Sir, I have plans to get some small pieces finished and available for purchase during Passover. That's always a busy time around here, right?"

"Yes," he grumbled, "but that's not definite enough. A good idea, but not a solid plan! You will build what WE say for you to build. We need help and you are prefect for the job. You got yourself into this mess, and if you want to get yourself out, you will follow OUR rules. Between you and me, I think they will forgive the debt, if you'll just go with their ideas Maccabee."

"Yes Sir!! No problem," I agreed out of fear!.

"Well, we need crosses for the crucifixions. Take what scrap lumber you find and get them done. They don't have to look pretty. It's not an attractive site but a necessary part of our job. Criminals are to be persecuted, and we, the Roman Soldier, has vowed to protect the people. We see that our city is safe and Caesar is given his due honor. Thieves aren't welcome here and will not be tolerated. That's what YOU are, when you don't pay your bills. Get to work, and I want it done by Thursday. I will bring a carriage to pick them up. Everything should be over by late Friday, and YOU can clean up the mess. They will have to be disposed of by The Sabbath. After all, it's your old lumber; and you do realize we are doing you a favor right?"

"Yes Sir!! No problem," again I timidly agreed.

Whew... There is a bit of relief in the opportunity to pay what I owe and this debt be eliminated for good. Yet, something about this just doesn't seem right. These men will hang on MY cross. Oh, I know, wrong should be punished, but I wonder who they are. I wonder if they are truly guilty? Between you and me, I'm not sure the Roman government is always exactly fair.

Oh well, it is what it is. I have a family to support, and I WILL DO JUST THAT and be grateful for this break. Now, off to the house to share the good news and get busy with the task at hand. If I do a good job on these, guaranteed income would be great. I will make this soldier happy and then we will talk about a contract for ALL the crosses they need. My dear wife has done without long enough. This could be HUGE for my family. Our best years are yet to come. I can feel it in my bones... There is a feeling of excitement and drive inside that has been gone for such a long time. I remember the motivation from that little baby so many years ago.

It's like He is somewhere close. I can feel His presence, but I'm not sure why.

I'll never forget that baby and the kindness in the eyes of His mother. I think her name was Mary. That's right. It was Mary and Joseph. Joseph was a carpenter too, and he complimented my cradle. That made me feel SO special since he was older than me.

AT LAST, THE CROSSES ARE COMPLETED AND PICKED UP!

Just one more task and I will be debt free. The soldier, Dave, and I made a pact on that! This will happen one charge at a time.

I can't imagine the pain the crucified men go through. This hill is tough enough to climb when you are fit and NOT carrying anything but a few tools. They said one of the men was beaten unmercifully, and then he was made to carry His cross up this hill. Oh, how I hope someone helped him. He is the one hung in the middle. I'm not sure what crime He committed. They say the other two were thieves. Boy, does that hit way too close to home!

I'm just ready to finish my part of this duty and get back home before the downpour. The loud thunder and blackness we had earlier today was weird. It came out of nowhere. A storm could definitely be brewing and I don't want to get caught in it.

WHAT DO YOU KNOW? One criminal has already been removed. The cleanup shouldn't take quite as long as I expected. I can take that cross down while the executioners finish breaking the legs of the others and then get those down.

I see Dave, the soldier, I've made this deal with him. He doesn't look quite as angry as before. Maybe this has gotten some pressure off his back too. It looks like he is kneeling at the foot of the empty cross. Maybe he has lost something. I will see if I can help. Or, should I give that criminal's mother some time alone before I interrupt? I assume that's His mother's lap they have laid him in, but she is REALLY young! She is like MY age. My kids are grown, but not the age of the guy that died. I will wait for her to say good-bye.

She looks a little familiar. I wonder if she has purchased furniture in the past? She may have been one of the ladies my wife has cooked for too. Who knows? I just don't understand why she keeps looking up at me and then down to her son. Should I know HIM?

Her eyes... So tender... So gentle.... I've seen those soft eyes before. I know... She looks like the girl at our stable when I was a kid. I built a cradle and gave...

THAT'S MARY HOLDING THAT MAN!!.....
Baby Jesus????? I built His cradle and now…

Mary held her baby,
Cradeled there so meek and small.
Surrounded only by the darkness,
Knowing not the road ahead.

Love so tender, there she pondered
The little man within her arms.
She'd protect him from all danger.
Harm can't reach that manger bed.

As He grew, she watched him stumble
But, she was there to break the falls.
Kiss the hurts, the bumps and bruises
He knew just who to call.

Once the young boy reached the temple,
Elders, priests…they were amazed.
It was as if he knew the Father,
Something they had never seen.

As He studied, many marveled
Baby boy no longer He.
He's about His Father's business.
Mary knew not what would be.

Still protecting from all danger.
And from the storms when they would come.

Then one day, He heard the Father
Saying "Now, this is your time.
Start there at river Jordan.
There's a hill that you must climb.

Heal the sick and some will love you.
Cast out demons in my name.
Then one day, they will take you.
I will be there through Your pain."

Then one day she saw them grab Him.
As a criminal, He was tried.
They judged Him and they lied.

Scorned and beaten, bruised and bleeding.
She could only watch as He walked by.
The heavy cross upon His shoulders,
Up Calvary's hill, and there to die.

Still, she wanted to protect Him
From the storms that now had come.
Through her tears,
She felt the anguish,
Heaven's work must now be done.

Then at last, the pain was over.
"It is finished," there He cried.
Then in her arms they finally laid Him.
Her little man had died.

Once again, she remembered
That little baby in her arms.
It wasn't meant that she protect Him.
For the Father had a plan.
She let Him go…
The task completed.
Salvation's peace to every man.

This is what all the talk had been about in town.
Jesus, that little baby Jesus, is the King they were
hailing in that parade last week. I knew there was
something special about Him. All the talk about
Him having disciples and teaching about God the
Father…IT WAS REAL!! What have I done? I
just built a cross for a man that had no reason to
die! I might as well have been the one who drove
the nails. Is that why the soldier is still there….
weeping? Does he feel the same guilt I am feeling?
What did he see in Jesus eyes as he crucified Him?

I must go talk with him, and hear what he has
to say about all this.

As I remember, these were the soldier's words.

I held Him there, as I drove the nails so deeply,
Yet thru the pain, my Lord forgave me.
I held Him there, and as He hung my burdens lightened.
His eyes met mine, but hurt I did not see.
As I held Him there, I heard, " My child, I love you.
And trust in Me will set your spirit free."

So…Then and there,
My life was changed completely.
With tear stained eyes, I bowed before my Lord.
Yes, I held Him there
But that's NOT the story's ending
For in that cross I found my blessed reward.

We can't drown in our own guilt that put Jesus on the cross. It was part of God's plan of redemption from the beginning of time. Yes, God's plan was that the life of His only begotten son begin at the cradle and continue til death on a Roman cross. Oh, it may have not been a boy named Maccabee that nailed the wood together, but someone may have built a cradle, and someone definitely built the cross.

His love beyond measure was made known to us that day. No matter the guilt that you have, no matter the depth of your sin and mine…His love, His flowing blood can wash that away. He doesn't want us to stay with Him in the cradle or on the cross. HE IS NO LONGER THERE!!! You see, just as the wood of the cradle is empty in Bethlehem...

Well, the wood of the cross is empty and removed from Calvary's hill.

Once again there is soooo much more to this life or should I say death? Yes, the sky turned black. God the Father turned His face away. It seemed this was the end.

They removed His body and laid Him in a borrowed tomb. All hope seemed lost.

HE ISN'T IN THE CRADLE! HE ISN'T ON THE CROSS! AND... HE ISN'T IN THE BORROWED TOMB!

Death has been conquered. His death on a cross IS our death to sin. Don't stop with the beauty of the cradle. Don't even stop with the amazing love displayed on a Roman cross.

All was not gained in Bethlehem, but all was not lost at Calvary!

HE WENT FROM CRADLE TO CROSS FOR YOU!!!

Bring Him Your Gift

There was a special night so long ago,
An infant child was born.
The stench of a barnyard stable
Became the baby's throne.

Mother and Father, ever so proud
Of this infant meek and mild.
Holy was the evening,
And yes, holy was the child.

A birthday yes, but not so pleasant.
One would wonder who He was.
A star shone high above Him
Even angels sang "Gloria."

He was King from the very beginning.
Some knew that from the start.
They came from nearby pastures
And even traveled from afar.

Shepherds brought Him nothing,
They had nothing for to give;
But the baby smiled at them gently
Looking up from Mother's arms.

She told them, "His name is Jesus,
Our family's so glad you came."

Magi traveled from distant lands
They brought gifts of greatest worth.
They came to pay him homage
And honor this special birth.

They bowed and presented treasures
In their robes of royal hue.
One would think that a magic moment;
But Jesus slept right through!

Mary told them, "His name is Jesus
Our family's so glad you came."

Mary handled all with gentleness.
You see, she was chosen by our Lord
To birth this babe, Emmanuel.
"God with us" from the start.

"Highly favored," were Gabriel's words.
But Mary's role so hard to play.

This was only the beginning.
The dawning of a brand new day.

I have to think others visited,
Some brought gifts… other's none.
Who knows the story's truth
Even a drummer may have come.

Yet, what might he have to offer?
Just a dirty little lad.
Possibly the strangest of all the guest;
From the streets and so poorly clad.

He wanted a gift so badly
To share with the special Babe.
With nothing to give and homeless
In desperation he came.

A toy drum made of sheep skin
Stretched across a piece of wood.
The instrument of both king and pauper
Sharing rhythm as only he could.

Softly he played for Jesus.
Can't you see the baby looking up?
The drummer boy looking back at him
With a smile and so much love.

Mary and Joseph must have been smiling too
As the little boy played on.
Then he lay the drum at Jesus feet...
Then nestled beside Him in the straw.

For the first time in such a long time,
The little lad was warm.
It seemed he had a family now,
And a shelter in the storm.

That gift, it seemed so small
But it was all he had to give.
When down to nothing, he gave his heart.
See, that's the difference for us all.

Orphaned and homeless we often wonder
The streets of our own Bethlehem.
Cold and hungry, tired and lonesome.
Til we find the Master's plan.

He wanted so badly to give something and couldn't think of anything; so, he just played for Him. Rhythm.... That's a gift! I've seen folks dancing that had NO rhythm. Haven't you? Point made! That was and still is a gift. The little drummer boy didn't think he had a gift to bring, so he simply played for the baby.

You see, that same baby boy, Jesus, became a man. He still allows us to bring any and all that we have to him. Not necessarily a wrapped gift for a newborn, but we present the gifts of our praise... our joys... our treasures... and yes... even our pain.

As the man Jesus grew, he offered Himself to the Father and we must do the same. Hanging from a Roman cross, Jesus drew His last breath for you and for me. The love He poured out, covered all the mistakes, sin, and hurt that we will ever bear. However, that grace... that love, can only be found when we give Him our heart which is OUR ULTIMATE GIFT!!

It really doesn't matter what gift you may have in the eyes of the world. It doesn't matter if you are labeled talented or not. The beauty of YOUR GIFT is determined by our Savior, when He alone looks deep into the heart of His children.

It's like the ugly Thanksgiving turkey a child makes with his hand. They bring it home to Mom and Dad smiling from ear to ear. Pretty??? NOPE!! Was it beautiful to Mom and Dad? YES!!! Why, because as parents, we looked into the heart of the giver. We saw OUR child and that gave the "ugly" paper turkey more value than one can imagine.

Our Heavenly Father feels the same way. When we have given Him our hearts, He can use every other part of our being for the glory of His kingdom.

Remember, "It takes a village" to raise a child. Well, God the Father has chosen you and me to be His hands and feet here on earth. We are the village chosen to share His love to a lost and fallen world. Yes, the King of all ages wants to use YOU and ME to do His work. He will show you your gift. Whatever it is, it's put in place for His glory… for His good… for His purpose!

At Christmas, sneak away,
Find you a closet to pray.
Keep the lights down low
And close the door behind you.
Unwrap all that hides within
And to your Father be true.

Get rid of all the garland.
There's no need for paper or bows.
Dig way down deep inside.
Confession is good for the soul.

You may want to bend a knee
To the One who gave it all.
He promised to ALWAYS listen.
That's the ONLY ONE to call.

What a perfect time and season
To launch a brand new start.
At Christmas… bring Him YOUR gift.
Give Him all your heart!

IF THE STABLE COULD SPEAK

Here we go again;
Every day the same.
I'm here to only shelter,
And sometimes house the lame.
No one cares about me.
The shepherds don't give a rip.
Bringing their herds for a moment,
Then they're off to higher plains.

Oh sure, when the weather is bad,
Back to me they run.
When the heat so intense they're wilting,
Yep, I'm their shelter from the sun.

I feel special for a little while,
But, who am I trying to fool?
There they go.
I probably won't see them again
Til they need refuge from the snow.

It would be nice to house something special.
In my mind, I play that game.
But, I just sit here a nobody.
My story, always the same.

Who would want to stay in stink?
Foul and filthy me.
I have little attraction
In a world so wild and free.

The mire that covers my floor
No one cares to clean.
I've only a tad of hay to share
Left by the very last team.

Travelers at times appreciate my grime.
For they're desperate and passing thru.
I get so excited. Then, off they go.
Fading away with morning's dew.

Yes, they leave behind more stench.
Maybe that's my problem.
If I could? If I were prettier?
Would my life not be so solemn?

I could clean the nasty ground,
And replace the broken lumber.

Wipe the cob webs from the ceiling
Shovel *"that stuff"* until I slumber.

If I were more attractive,
Maybe guests would spend more time.
Shepherds might see my value
And take pride in how I shine.

Then, just maybe, I could house the best.
They would bring me a newborn calf
To nestle and to hold.
Wouldn't it be special
To shelter beauty from the cold?

If I got all squeaky clean,
I could do a better job.
I'd offer unsoiled straw for feed
They would know I'd been redeemed.

That's exactly what I'll do!
Tomorrow I begin anew.
I will change from the inside out,
And be ready for the crew.

Tonight I'll rest and clear my mind
I'll conquer this massive feat.
I'll go from worthless to great value

When I'm done,
A change you'll see.

It's super late,
So I'm calling it a day.
I'll rest up for the plan ahead.
The next herd will be impressed
With clean straw and an unsoiled bed.

What? A couple staying here? Tonight? I had plans tomorrow to get some things done. Travelers are here again to further trash my stall and then be on their way. From the looks of the lady, it doesn't appear she planned this little excursion very well. She looks exhausted and might I add miserable. At least they only have one animal to foster the aroma that dwells within these walls. Couldn't they have waited until I could tidy up just a bit? I would have been proud to house the overflow from the inn if the boss had given me a little heads up about his plan. I mean really. I'm used to animals, but PEOPLE! I'm definitely not equipped for them out here.

They must be really desperate! Wow... She looks desperate in more ways than one! It's clear they won't be here long. She will need way more help than I can offer.

I suppose the best I can do is apologize for the way I am and try to be polite. They are probably less than excited to bed down in these confines. Maybe when they go inside for the evening meal with the other residents, I can shovel out the worst of the *"you know what"* and they will at least have a dry place to rest their weary and blossoming bodies.

They are headed back.
I've only a little done.
To replace the stench I harbor
And be ready for someone.

I'm never good enough for much,
Yet seldom needed for little more,
Adequate, but only barely;
Just canopy, walls and floor.

The calm outside so strange.
Just an owl howls in the distance.
My boarders fast asleep.
I think I'll bed down with them.
"Good night."

What's that in the heavens?
It's such an amazing star!
I hear a baby gently crying.
And a huge celestial choir.

Glory to God in the highest?
Is that what they are singing?
Something has changed inside me.
I sparkle, my floors they're gleaming!

Oh my… this baby is like glowing!
The man called his lady "Mary."
She is talking to her husband.
The babe is born that she once carried.

I just heard her call him "Jesus."
There's something special about that name.
His presence seems woven inside my walls.
I don't think I'll ever be the same.

Just His presence now within me
As she strokes His gentle face.
Something about His spirit.
Has brought awe into this place.

I've tried for oh so many years
To change what was marred and shattered.
But on my own, an impossible task.
I'd never understood
What really and truly mattered.

I find myself shouting
To all who are passing by.

"Do you see my baby?
Come on, come see inside.

I'm different since He came.
He's cleaned me. I'm complete!!
Come everyone, see my baby.
I now have shelter for the weak."

I heard the couple talking.
She said that He's a King!
He will save the nation Israel.
"I have a song to sing!"

What a peaceful time for me.
Resting in all that love.
The gift of His holy presence
Sent from up above.

Soon the precious family left me.
They had room for them inside.
Mary really needed better provisions.
So she and Baby Jesus would thrive.
It's ok. I have my story.
For the first time I'm alive!

T'was no need to clean up first.
Somehow, Jesus did that for me.
I can't explain just how it happened,

But one thing I know for sure.
I'm no longer burdened by guilt.
I'm extra special and now you see.
All is washed and wiped away.
I have truly been set free.

Yes, at times I still get a little messy.
That's ok.
For my heart is what really matters.
I have purpose now,
And joy unending,
He has made beauty from the tatters.

I want to speak to each one passing.
"Do you know my Jesus?"
Let me tell you about my friend.
I'm changed from the inside out.
He made me new again.

When you come to know my Jesus
You too can share His peace.
"Come here, let me tell you.
Won't you hear my story please?"

He transformed me so completely.
He can do the same for you.
He'll clean your heart, satisfy your soul…
Won't you let Him be YOUR LORD!

You see, this little baby,
They call Him Immanuel.
God with us is what they're saying.
We've all a story to tell.

Silence is not option
When He truly lives inside.
Share His love to everyone.
Make YOUR story come alive.

Tell what He has done for you!!
Give Him all credit due.
Bring others to His stable
So their lives can be complete.
They too, can be set free!

Witnesses say He grew
And later died.
He hung on a cross for me.
I can't imagine the pain of that.
It took place on Calvary.

His blood washed away my sin,
Just like my stable came clean.
I'll never have to fear those stains
For I have been redeemed.

It's All About The Baby

The hustle and bustle of the season,
Well, it's upon us once again.
I've a ton of decorating
Hanging garland strand by strand.

Folks in town are singing carols.
There is a group on every street.
They smile and offer greetings.
"Merry Christmas
And on earth… peace."

There's our tree and all its glory
In the window standing huge.
It makes one wonder from the outside
What is under the branches true.

There are gifts like you just can't imagine.
They cover the entire floor!

From toys to the latest device;
You can hardly open the door!

The hallway takes the overflow.
The train whistles round the track.
Around again.... Then back.

I've even MORE shopping to do now,
Another guest was added to the list!
Just spending money right and left,
Of course, more than those "wallet and tie" gifts.

"Honey, do this and that.
Get this place ready to impress the world!"
Trimming the house with lights full circle,
And yard ornaments now unfurled.

Then, there's the groceries I will purchase.
We will have a feast!
I'm not sure what the neighbors are eating.
All wrapped up in their Christian beliefs.

They have only a tiny manger scene.
It sets centered in their yard.
You'd think they would be more impressive.
After all... There is a sub-division reward.

What a prestigious honor it is
To have the most beautiful house.
We should win the prize hands down.
And we will be the talk of the town.

I'll raise my glass at the meeting.
Everyone will know my name.
Then they will all share the pictures,
And next year... their houses will look the same.

What more could there be for this holiday?
Like they say... "family, gifts and fun."
But then in a few short minutes.
Everything is done.

Now... it is upon us.
Tomorrow is the big day.
I'll manage to get all tasks completed,
But I just wished the kids would go play.

My nerves are at their end!
My once clean house a mess.
I need to find some calm,
A place of peace and rest.

When we are finished with the presents
And the holiday meal is served, I'll get away,

Just take a little stroll
To calm these shattered nerves.

It's off to bed for the littles,
Their heads swimming with delight.
Another night cap for the bigger kids
And last minute wrapping gifts up tight.

"Good Morning! Merry Christmas!"
A joyful greeting from toddler to foe.
The gifts are perfect for each, of course.
Torn paper tossed to and fro.

It is so special watching the children;
Their innocence such a joy.
They are gleaming with excitement
Then quickly on to another toy.
Today is made so special.
Just seeing their smiling faces.
Being a grandmother does soften the heart.

However, my fuse is growing shorter.
It's time to take that walk.
Fun and family overload I think.
I don't even want to talk.

Just a little time to wonder.
I need to get away.

When my nerves are somewhat settled, I'll return.
To "wrap up" this holiday.

The clean brisk air is calming
And distant sounds ring out.
Wandering closer, they are clearer.
Chimes so soft and gentle,
As if they are reaching out.

I seemed to be drawn to them.
Mystified by their tone.
Overtaken by their spirit.
I'm surrounded, yet alone.

I entered into this little church.
That's the first time I'd heard the bells.
They rang amid the chaos.
And it seemed they called my name.

As I stumbled down the aisle,
Still weary from the shopping lure,
In the empty darkened building,
I began my personal tour.

Only one beam shone like starlight.
It was way up in the front.
Streaming through the stained glass window,
I saw a pile of hay and stuff.

"What in the world," I thought.
Who would have made this nasty mess?
It's like some play was over,
And here lay all the rest.

Apalled, I began to straighten a little.
This was just not right!
Something must be done,
But this could take me half the night.

Boards were scattered and cluttered
In an otherwise well-kept place.
Then amid the rubble and the brightest light …
A cloak of white; and a tiny face.

It was then I heard a noise and he appeared.
His voice one of calm and peace.
"Can I help you Miss, are you lost?
You are welcome to have a seat."

I explained, I needed nothing,
But had heard the lovely bells.
He said, "Yes, they rang throughout the day today
For the world to know His birth."
His birth??? I thought… What on earth???

Then I saw his face.

It was my neighbor....the religious one
With the manger scene in his yard.
I wanted to run, for I'm not always friendly,
But was captured and felt disgraced.

Since no escape was to be had,
I listened to him explain.
He told the story that I'm sure you've heard
Of the baby that now there lay.

He told me about a virgin birth;
One that would astound.
Absolutely NOTHING he said made sense,
Yet I believed his every word.
It was the most beautiful story
That I had ever heard.
Then he asked if I knew this Jesus.
And I had to answer "No."

So there in that starlit empty church,
I finally understood.
I'd had it oooooh so wrong.
All the pieces fit together now,
The emptiness, gone for good.

This baby Jesus came for me
Way back then, in Bethlehem.

Then walked a lonely road and died.
To forgive every last one of my sins.

I'd never known this kind of love
That had now been born in me.
It has nothing to do with gifts and tinsel
Around a Christmas tree!

Needless to say,
My nerves then settled
So I returned,
To that once chaotic home.
I shared a story of bells from an empty church
And of the Savior and His birth.

Christ is what makes Christmas.
I was so blind but now I see.
"Father, give me a heart to share Your word.
For others to be set free."

How could I have missed the point
For oh, so many years?
On my knees, that day, my life was changed.
And now flow my happy tears.

If you know someone wrapped up in "stuff" this
Christmas,
Let them know the truth!

I'll join you in praying for them,
That their heart will be made new.

A story but so much more.
To the world, it just might seem crazy;
But oh, the joy in finally understanding...
IT'S ALL ABOUT THE BABY!!

.

JESUS, THE LIGHT OF THE WORLD

O h, the joys of being a shepherd boy......
Joys??? Did I say joys??? Actually, there's
nothing special about this life. And to top it off,
as the youngest kid, I always have to work the left
over shifts. This is getting old, and I'm not even
sixteen yet.

But Dad, I just worked last night.
Can't Ben go out and help?
He never wants to pitch in
And only thinks about himself.

Sorry David, since you're the youngest.
That's just the way it is.
The older boys have seniority,
When it comes to all of this.

Tonight, you'll have a helper
Just in case the weather is bad.

49

Aaron can assist in herding,
So you can take a nap.

Be sure to keep an eye out
Since the wolves have been about.
No nodding through the night ya know.
Sleep will come with morning's light.

Walk on now, Son.
Do the very best that you can.
One day, you'll be proud of all you've done.
Hard work always pays off… Just believe.

Here's an extra energy drink,
To keep you wide awake.
Drink it now and stay alert,
No need to take a break.

Be sure to take your cell phone
And do make sure it's charged.
No surfing on the job ya know.
Batteries only last so long.

Now, go on out just like I said.
You've been chosen for tonight.
An evening off is coming soon.
I promise to make things right.

Aaron said he'd help you out
I've told him exactly what to do.
Put a smile on your face now kiddo.
There's no need to be so blue.

Well, I did as I was told;
But, with an attitude I might add!
This life just really stinks
For an up and coming lad!

Another night… another howl…
Another "not so bright" sheep.
Ya gotta leave the ninety and nine,
When that foolish one takes a leap.

They aren't the smartest animals alive.
Oh, the choices that they make.
They will leave a perfectly good pasture and
journey off.
It's often a huge mistake.

Why on earth would one wander
From the safety of the shepherd's fold?
Why won't they just listen,
And do as they are told?

I'm here for their protection.
Their shepherd is one they can trust.

Yet, they often drift away
To find comfort in other lusts.

Oh well, I'd better brace for rain.
The clouds are rolling in.
When the storms start 'round here,
We run for an open den.

Of course, Aaron is fast asleep.
Sure hope he gets his rest.
He did nothing more than what Dad told him,
Leaving me to finish the rest.

Feed, water and check the lambs.
All ewes and bucks now accounted for.
Surely, I can at least check emails
Before sunrise knocks upon the door.

There is thunder in the distant west,
Yet billows are breaking in the north.
They seem completely lifted due east.
I pray for a calm and silent night,
Oh, and just a little warmth.

Nothing ever changes.
All my nights here are the same.
Take captive all the predators,
Mend the torn, and tend the lame.

The newest lamb today is crippled.
One back leg just isn't right.
He is ever so determined though.
His heart is full of fight.

I worked with him and shaped a splint.
It's perfect for his little leg.
So thankful he didn't seem to be in pain.
He's laying here beside me now
Just in case of rain.

With me here as their shepherd,
There's really nothing they should need.
They can take rest in the greenest pastures.
And by still waters they will feed.

Just before dawn is the hardest time,
To keep from a little slumber.
Aaron's snoring will help in that.
It's worse than the early thunder.

Oh, to dose and dream a bit
Of the days when I am older.
I'd like to imagine a different time.
Filled with awe and wonder.

Surely, there is something out there
To brighten up my days.

"The light at the end of a tunnel," they say,
"Is not always an oncoming train."

Daddy says there's a Messiah coming
But how would that spread delight?.
How could that help a shepherd boy?
And change this lonely life?

Oh, what a beautiful peaceful darkness!
A chorus of locusts buzz.
There's something special in the air.
This night so calm and rare.

"AARON, AARON…..WAKE UP!!"

"DAVID, GET THAT FLASHLIGHT OUT OF MY EYES RIGHT NOW!"

"BUT AARON, GET UP! THAT'S NOT MY FLASHLIGHT! Look! I've never seen anything like this. That star!! That star goes all the way from the ground to the top of the heavens! It's like it's touching the land way down the road towards Bethlehem. AARON…. IT'S BEAUTIFUL. LET'S GO SEE!!"

"Please David… Really? Leave me alone already!

Wow…. That really is bright;
And not so far away.

And do you hear those voices?
Is that coming from the sky?"

"I thought you were still sleeping, Aaron.
It's about time you saw.
I've been watching this for hours,
And now it's nearly dawn.

I can't believe you didn't hear the choir.
Thousands of angels singing praise.
They sang, "Glory to God in the highest."
Every voice perfectly raised.

And that star, it hasn't dimmed
Yet it dances brightly in the sky
Like it's enticing us to follow.
Come on…. You want to try?"

"David, you can't FOLLOW A STAR!
You know better than that.
There are times the "little brother" in you really shows.
What happens if we get off track?

And the sheep, they need a shepherd
They could mix with another flock.
Dad would be so angry,
And then our pay would be docked!

"Oh, come on Aaron just this once.
Let's see where that star is leading.
I'll take this cripple with me
In case it needs more treatment.

The rest of the herd will be fine.
They are still all bedded down.
There's not one coyote howling out there.
That choir is the only sound.

Jacob and the others are sure to be here soon.
They'll see that all is well.
You never know what we may find.
That star could have a story to tell."

Well, we gathered up the coolers
And I bundled up my little lamb.
Aaron decided to join me
As this life changing journey began.

We traveled through the morning
Then stopped to eat a bite.
This trip changed greatly with every step,
As we grew closer to the light.
Even after the sun began rising in the East.
It still glistened ever so bright.

A voice inside me kept calling
"Come and follow me."
The light penetrated my very soul.
And by its radiance I could see.
I saw way down deep inside;
Things that didn't make me proud.
How I'd just argued with my Dad.
It had gotten pretty loud.

I began to examine my heart.
What in the world was going on?
Where were these thoughts coming from?
It was ONLY a pretty star.

"Aaron, do you feel ok?
Anything you want to say?
There's something different about this trip
Even if it's not far away."

My heart began beating faster
It's like a change is taking place.
I'm drawn closer to the glow
With each step I speed my pace.

Hope stirs deep inside me,
And there's a freedom I've never known.
This light is pointing to a better way
From this darkness where I've roamed.

I wished everyone we knew were with us.
To find the true meaning of this light.
Somehow, it's not just a star we follow,
But a chance to make things right.

"Hurry Aaron, let's go faster.
We can take turns carrying the lamb.
I just gotta see what's up there.
It's really special, I can tell.

Can you hear that? There's still singing.
Now, I see angels in the sky.
"In excelsis deo"
Is that the chorus they're chanting?"

I've got to hurry,
We're getting closer.
Bethlehem is just up the road.
It seems to hoover just outside of town.
Beside the land that Daddy sold.

There's nothing there but an empty stable
Where we took shelter now and then.
I remember taking the animals inside,
Since we didn't have any pens.

The man that bought the property
Was going to tear it down.

He said it was only an eye sore
For visitors coming into town.

It's definitely nothing special.
There's nothing there to sing about.
"Let's go around the back side
Like we did when we were little.
With the taxing going on,
Then, we'll avoid the crowds."

As we came all the closer to the light,
My heart raced with a strange excitement.
I knew my life would be transformed.
Like the sky, my heart enlightened.

We sorta sneaked around the back.
Where we used to run and play.
Even the morning sun didn't cover that star
As we quickly made our way.

Then, there as we emerged from the woods
The broken lamb within our arms,
A glow like I've never seen before…
Right above the barn!

Well, "barn" may not be exactly right,
'Twas more like a "stall" in the roughest sense.

Then beneath that light a family huddled
And there a newborn baby, by its mother, snuggled.

We then walked slowly toward them.
The infant lying sweetly in her arms.
Cuddled there in these surroundings;
Yet, peaceful, beautiful and warm.

They invited us in their little home,
And we joined them to celebrate.
So grateful for the meager stall
Since they had arrived so late.

"Mary" was the lady's name
But she was little more than a girl.
"Joseph," her husband as I recall
And the baby "Jesus"...
Well, he had surely changed their world!

It was then I realized again
The star that we had followed
Shining brightly overhead.
I began to recall the prophet's account
Of a Savior that would come.
"Messiah" as my Daddy said.
Could this be the one????

The love within that simple shed
Was more than words can say.
This was it!
The stories I'd heard
Had all come true that day.

Right there before my eyes,
Was the mighty Prince of Peace.
A light was then born within me
For all the world to see.

Wow... just a shepherd boy tending sheep
On a night like all the rest.
I'd be chosen to see the Christ child,
And share with you how I'd been blessed.

I knelt and tears ran down my face.
The Savior Christ was born.
I lay that tiny lamb before him
Though splinted and a somewhat torn.

That little lamb was all I'd brought.
So I placed it before the King.
His throne was a tiny manger bed.
My heart began to sing.

I want to tell each one of you
His light within you can shine.

There's a world out there that needs Him.
In so many ways… they are blind.

Go share this light and spread His love.
The season for you will change.
Christmas will hold a new meaning
You will never be the same.

David had a story
To share to all the world.
And you….
You have a story too.

If you know this Jesus,
Well, there's your story.
If you don't,
Now is the time.
Open your heart to the light of the world.
Tiny baby, yet divine.

You hold this special light inside
Turn it on and let it shine.
Take it with you every day
Share it with all mankind.

ABOUT THE AUTHOR

R uby McGuill grew up in Edna, Texas and has always had a love for music and writing. She began writing poetry and studying piano and voice as an elementary student. At ten years old, she gave her heart to Christ and at twelve, Ruby accepted her first position as church pianist at Morales Baptist Church just outside her hometown. She attended Wharton County Junior College before relocating to the Houston area.

Ruby moved back to South Texas and married Grady Pat McGuill in 1987 and joined him in service in the Catholic Church in 1989. After a few short years, they moved to Lexington, Texas where she continued to work in local churches. She has been the accompanist for La Grange First United Methodist Church chancel choir for over 10 years, and for various other congregations in the area. After 26 years, they are excited to have recently moved to La Grange, Texas. Ruby is also a graphics artist for L. W. Stolz Memorials, Inc. in La Grange.

Grady and Ruby have two adult children. Sean is a graduate of Northwestern State University in Natchitoches, Louisiana with a degree in General Studies and a focus on music. Kathlyn is a 2014 graduate of Texas A&M University in College Station, Texas where she majored in Sociology with a minor in music.

"One of my greatest blessings was to serve on the music team for a Holy Rosary ACTS Retreat." It was during her first team retreat in April 2012 that she felt the call to broaden this ministry. "God has opened doors of opportunity and with faith and excitement I will follow in whatever direction He leads. Ruby McGuill Ministries was laid on my heart and God has blessed it by providing bookings and travel to several areas across Texas and Oklahoma." Ruby shares a music program coupled with some of the stories contained in these pages. Another branch of her ministry is the creation of an inspirational